3 Values of Being an Effective Person

By Eric Papp

3 VALUES OF BEING AN EFFECTIVE PERSON BY
ERIC PAPP

ISBN: 978-0-9965217-0-3
Copyright © 2015 by Eric Papp
Cover design by: Ilian

For more information on this book and the author visit:
www.ericpapp.com.

Printed in the United States of America.

Dedication

To my beautiful wife, Brieann. Thank you for saying "Yes."
May we both honor our word, take responsibility, and give generously to each other and everyone we encounter.

Table of Contents

Introduction

What are the standards of behavior for yourself and your organization?

I recently had a meeting with some leaders of a company. When I walked into their corporate office, they had their seven values on the wall: Integrity, Service, Quality, Team, Commitment, Respect, and Communication.

When we met in the board room, I asked them . . .

What are the values of your organization?

They knew some of them but sent someone to get the full list of seven. I then asked them . . .

Do you know the behavior that represents each value?

They each gave me a different answer.

Even if people know the values of an organization, there is a great chance they have **conflicting behaviors**.

Values are the **foundation** of leadership. They are the standards of behavior.

Values = Standards of Behavior

The standard of behavior in most organizations comes from what we see other people do.

BOSS THAT MICROMANAGES

LACK OF TRUST AND COMMUNICATION

Most organizations have competing standards of behavior and are **delusional** in thinking their folks actually practice their values.

When I was in the Boy Scouts, we had the Scout Law.

A scout is trustworthy, loyal, helpful, friendly, courteous, kind, obedient, cheerful, thrifty, brave, clean, and reverent.

That was our standard of behavior.

We recited it and talked about it at every meeting.

In most organizations, people are uncomfortable talking about values.

When we don't talk about them, we don't see them.

Talking about values (standards of behavior) has **nothing** to do with judgement; rather, it has everything to do with performance.

When we overcome the fear of talking about values at work, we shape ourselves and our organizations to the results we want to achieve.

Carpenters bend wood; fletchers bend arrows; wise men fashion themselves.
~ Buddha

After years of studying, observing, and teaching leadership, I have discovered **3 Values** that encompass what it means to **be** a leader.

3 Values of Being an Effective Leader:

Honesty: honoring your word and being honest with your opinions.

Responsibility: making it happen.

Generosity: giving without expectation.

The Model Explained

When you have a combination of someone who honors his word (honesty) and accepts
100 percent responsibility, the result is a transparent/authentic leader.

You see his strengths and weaknesses. There is no disconnect from what he says and does.

3 VALUES OF BEING AN EFFECTIVE PERSON

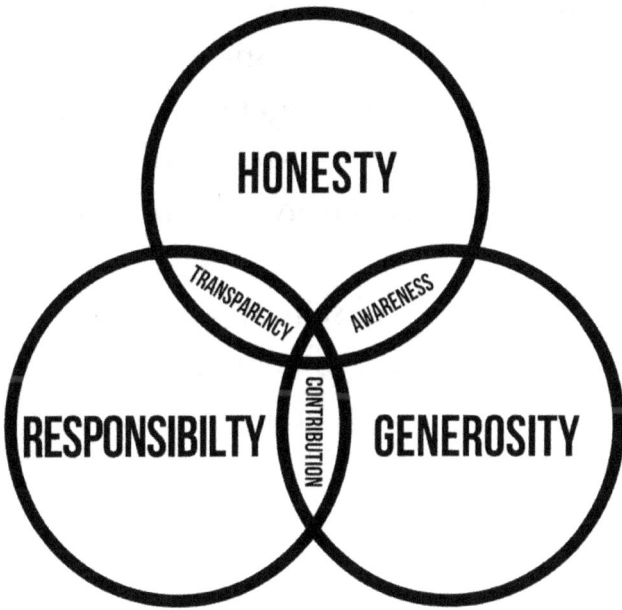

Eric Papp

When an individual is honest with his opinions of himself (**honesty**) and gives without expectation (**generosity**), there is a raised level of awareness of how his behavior is perceived by others.

A high level of self-awareness is an integral part of being effective with others.

When an individual gives without expectation (**generosity**) and takes on 100 percent responsibility, it allows for him to make a great contribution in whatever area he focuses.

The giving of oneself (**generosity**) demonstrates one of the most authentic actions leaders can take.

You'll see the distinction between self -sacrificing vs sacrificing others in this book.

Values and Behavior Disconnect

The disconnect between the values of an organization and the behavior of employees is the core of many problems such as: disengaged employees, poor performance, lack of accountability, and communication silos.

IF EVERYONE PRACTICED THE 3 VALUES
(STANDARDS OF BEHAVIOR) YOU WOULDN'T SPEND
TIME IN THE WEEDS.

Knowing Values vs Being the Values

If a new hire reads the organizational values, does that knowledge mean he will now practice them?

If someone takes a course on leadership, does that mean he will demonstrate leadership or fall back on authority?

Knowing leadership and being a leader
are two distinct concepts.

This book is about the **3 Values** of **being**
that allow for effective
leadership, and only work when
made into a daily habit.

*We are what we repeatedly do. Excellence
is not an act but a habit.*
~ Aristotle

When made into a habit, you gain
power, peace of mind, and an increase in
performance.

Too often, people confuse authority as leadership.

LEADERSHIP VS. AUTHORITY

WOULD PEOPLE STILL FOLLOW ME IF I DIDN'T HAVE MY POSITION/TITLE OR WEALTH?

Building your leadership on the foundation of these **3 Values** is like building your house on a solid foundation.

Acquiring more skills without a strong foundation is ineffective. It is often a waste of time and resources.

How effective is it to spend money on leadership skills when the foundation has cracks?

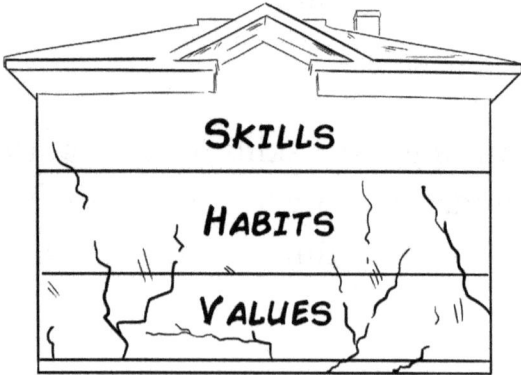

SKILLS

HABITS

VALUES

Stop spending resources on leadership skills and focus on establishing a strong foundation.

Most organizations today are suffering from problems with their foundation, yet they are remodeling the kitchen.

The foundation of leadership starts with our habitual behaviors.

Honesty
How effective will strategic thinking skills be if someone doesn't honor his word?

Responsibility
How effectively can someone build a team if she doesn't take responsibility?

Generosity
How effective are communication skills if we are not generous listeners?

Leadership is not complicated.
If it is, it's because
we created it that way.

Now, more than ever, we have hundreds of thousands of books on leadership, courses on ethics, and more leadership training than anyone can take in a lifetime.

Yet, there is still a leadership problem in most organizations . . . and homes.

Remember . . . it's not about how much you know.

Honesty
How many leadership courses did Abraham Lincoln take before he became known as Honest Abe?

Responsibility
How many leadership books did Gandhi read before he took on the responsibility of leading his people?

Generosity
How much leadership training did Mother Teresa receive before she started putting others before herself?

Being **honest**, **responsible**, and **generous** is like being on a treadmill. There is **no end**. It is an ongoing process, and you can control the **speed** and **degree** of the **treadmill.**

If these are to be the standards of your behavior, they must be practiced and talked about daily.

Nothing so conclusively proves a man's
ability to lead others
as what he does from day to day
to lead himself.
~ Thomas J. Watson

Please don't confuse the size of this book with the impact it can have on your life and your organization.

The Gettysburg Address was only 272 words and took less than three minutes.

Did you know Edward Everett was actually the featured speaker that day and spoke before Lincoln for over two hours?

Enjoy this book. At the end of each chapter, you'll have space to record your thoughts and questions to share with your team.

Part 1

What Matters in Leadership?

What Matters?

Two simple words that form a question and get right to the **core** of any conversation, problem, situation, or subject.

What matters in Leadership?

What matters to me is that you identify foundational concerns in your organization's leadership.

What Matters?

What matters to you in being
a leader?

Do your values reflect your behavior?

Would others say you have
authority or leadership?

What Matters?

What matters to me is that you'll be able
to improve your life by incorporating
the **3 values** of being an effective leader.

We can only improve when we look for
areas and when we are honest
with ourselves.

No self-examination . . . no
improvement.

What Matters?

Identifying what matters is your motivation to improve your leadership.

So . . . what matters to YOU?

1. _____

2. _____

3. _____

Is what matters to you **proportional** to how you spend your time?

HONEST WITH OURSELVES

MY TOP 2 PRIORITIES ARE MY FAITH & FAMILY

I DON'T HAVE TIME TO GO TO MATT'S GAME. I WORK FOR A LIVING. AND PLEASE STOP REMINDING ME ABOUT CHURCH

What Really Does Matter?

What Matters?

Why is there a vast **disconnect** between what we say **matters**, and where we actually spend our time?

Maybe we are not honest with ourselves.

What Matters?

Knowing vs. Being

How do we have so many books on leadership . . . and still lack leaders?

How can someone get a degree in leadership and still be viewed as an incompetent person?

What Matters?

How much does knowledge matter when it comes time for us to be effective?

How do we have so many overweight people when most of them know they need to exercise more and eat less?

How do we have so many books and courses on relationships and still have a divorce rate of 50 percent?

Disconnect?

Can you see the disconnect in
knowing vs being?

What matters to me is that you
become an effective leader.

We chase knowledge thinking it will
make the difference.

Sustainable Leadership

For about three years, I taught one and
two-day public seminars
on a variety of
management/leadership topics.

I was obsessed with the question . . .

*How much will be implemented
and sustainable?*

Strong Foundation

Leadership training is most effective when we have a strong foundation.

Without a strong foundation, learning leadership skills makes little impact.

Most organizations are wasting money putting leadership skills on a shaky foundation.

Weak Foundation...No Sustainability of Skills

Weak Foundation . . .
No Sustainability of Skills

Employees take leadership training, yet
can't incorporate the strategies because
their company
doesn't pull for it.

We learn by seeing the behavior
of others.

A majority of learned behavior takes
place on the job.

What Matters?

Are you seeing the **distinction** between knowing information and being effective?

Being an effective leader means establishing a strong foundation of behaviors and practicing them daily.

What Matters?

The old model in being a leader is to acquire more knowledge or authority.

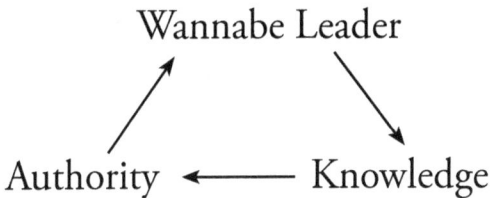

Wannabe Leader

Authority ← Knowledge

Let's promote the person with all the knowledge, certifications, and training.

What Matters?

We live in a world where we have vast
amounts of knowledge at our fingertips,
yet we still struggle
with effectiveness.

Effectiveness: the degree to which
something is successful in producing a
desired result.

What Matters?

A company's values on paper or the
behavior of its employees?

Expanded View

What matters is that this book expands your view of what it means to **be** a leader.

We are limited in situations by our perspective and old ways of thinking.

When we expand our view, we generate new ideas.

Expanded View

We cannot solve our problems with the same thinking we used when we created them.
~ Albert Einstein

Expanded View

A new view gives you access to new ideas. New ideas give you new action. New action provides a new level of performance.

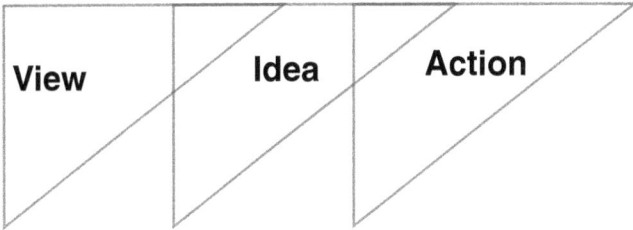

View   Idea   Action

This book is about giving you a new view on honesty, responsibility, and generosity.

Part 2

Being an Effective Leader . . . Honesty

Honesty

How do you view honesty?

How you view honesty determines how
you practice it.

Honesty

Being honest involves two parts:

Honoring your word. Promises you make to yourself and others.

Being honest in your opinions.

Honesty

At what degree do you honor your word?

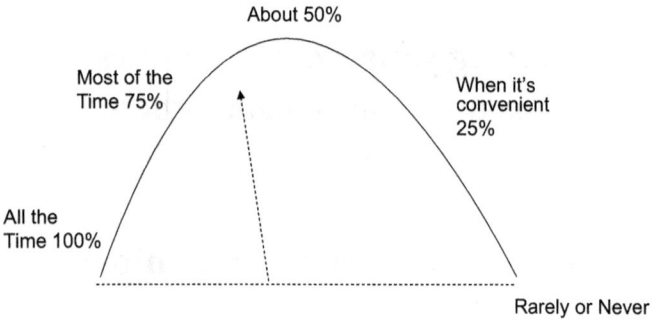

About 50%

Most of the
Time 75%

When it's
convenient
25%

All the
Time 100%

Rarely or Never

THE HANDSHAKE

WHAT HAPPENED TO THE TIME WHEN
THIS USED TO MEAN SOMETHING?

Honoring Your Word

Honoring your word—promises you make to yourself and others.

Honesty starts with promises we make to ourselves.

How effective are you at honoring the promises you make to yourself (i.e. "workout," "eating healthier," "write a book," etc.)?

Honoring Your Word

If we are making promises to ourselves
and not honoring them, there is a good
chance we are making promises to other
people and not honoring them.

This behavior is impacting our
performance, and we don't
even realize it.

Honoring Your Word

When you honor the promises you
make to yourself . . . you start to develop
self-trust.

The more we practice honoring our
word, the **stronger** it becomes.

Imagine saying, "I'm going to lose ten
pounds in five weeks,"
and it happens.

Remember the treadmill analogy?

Honoring Your Word

I promised to_____and fulfilled it.
I promised to_____and fulfilled it.
I promised to_____and fulfilled it.

I promised to_____; Life happened
and I didn't fulfill it.

Make a new promise and get back on
the treadmill.

Be a Person of Your Word

Be a Person of Your Word

You can't always keep your word.
Life happens.

When you can't honor your word,
communicate to all those involved and
restore it.

You restore it by making a new promise.

You'll feel relieved when you restore it—
not guilty.

Honor Your Word

When you honor your word, you are
viewed as trustworthy, and people will
follow you and listen to you.

When someone doesn't care about
honoring his word, he is unaware
of the impact.

THE IMPACT OF NOT HONORING YOUR WORD

Being an Effective Leader

Being honest in your opinions

Why most people are not honest:
Have you ever been to a restaurant and
said to yourself, "This food is
not that good, I've had better"?

And then the waitress or manager
shows up and asks, "How is
everything?"

What do most of us do?

Most of us would rather **lie** to someone
rather than tell her our
honest opinion.

*Honesty is an expensive gift; don't
expect it from cheap people.*
–Warren Buffett

How can we be more honest with
others?

Not Being Honest = Constant Source of Frustration

When we are not honest with our opinions or expectations, this can serve as a constant source of frustration.

Some managers aren't honest about their expectations of their employees. Instead of having an honest conversation, they will rationalize it by doing a cost/benefit analysis.

Not Being Honest = Constant Source of Frustration

When you have honest communication with others, you will feel powerful and relieved because you are being straight in your communication.

Honest in Your Opinions

Many of us are not honest about our opinions because of one of two reasons.

1. We don't like conflict, and we assume there will be conflict if we are honest.

2. We do a cost/benefit analysis.

"I don't want to mention how Nancy's negative attitude affects the team, since she is always to work on time."

Honest in Your Opinions

Being honest with our opinion is not
about making someone feel bad.

It's about having freedom in our
communication.

If you are worried someone will get
upset by your honesty,
preface it first.

"When can we have an honest
conversation about performance?"

Honest in Your Opinions

You don't need to be
brutally honest.

People who say, "I'll be brutally honest,"
tend to be more brutal than honest.

Practicing **gentle honesty** gives you the
freedom to respectfully express yourself
to others.

Honest in Your Opinions

When you're not honest in
communication, you have
limited depth.

A majority of conversations
lack depth.

Limited Honesty . . . Limited Depth

Limited Depth . . . Limited Trust

Limited Trust . . . Limited Relationship

WHAT LEVEL ARE MOST OF YOUR CONVERSATIONS?

FERTILIZER CONVERSATIONS = WEATHER, SPORTS AND NEWS

SOIL CONVERSATIONS = TALK ABOUT OTHER PEOPLE

CORE CONVERSATIONS = TALK ABOUT WHAT MATTERS AND HONEST IN OUR OPINIONS

Not Being Honest Impacts Performance

Prospect says: "Just send me a proposal."

Salesperson: "Sure thing."

Prospect has no intention of doing business but just wanted to quickly deal with the salesperson.
Salesperson wastes time compiling proposal and following up.

Honest salesperson: "Are you asking for a proposal because you are really interested?"

Being Honest

Do you find it difficult talking to someone about their performance?

What are the conversations about employee performance you need to have but have been procrastinating?

Honest in Your Opinions

Your employees are not
fragile people, so let's stop treating
them like that.

Being honest is about honoring our
word and being honest with
our opinions.

Remember . . . intent determines
approach.

Be **gently honest**—
not brutally honest.

Honesty

Some companies demonstrate a lack of honesty by not being transparent.

When companies withhold information, people create their own rumors.

When people create their own rumors, this creates confusion and impacts performance.

Honesty

Organizations should practice being transparent.

This is why there is a lack of trust between most employees and the organization they work for.

WE LIVE IN A GLOBAL TRANSPARENT WORLD

Honesty

Until we start to look and see where our promises to ourselves and others are falling short . . . our performance **will not** change.

Until we provide people with honest feedback, the performance of others will not change and we will continue to be frustrated.

Impact of Being Honest

When we make the choice to honor our
word, it causes us to be
more present in our conversations and
more aware of the
promises we make.

Many of us tend to be too casual in
promises we make, and we never intend
to fulfill them.

Impact of Being Honest

Every time we overcome the fear of
being honest with our opinions, we
increase our freedom of
self-expression and establish a deeper
relationship with someone.

Impact of Not Being Honest

When we are not honest with others we are being **inauthentic**.

Impact of Being Honest

Leaders who honor their word are
transparent in their
words and actions.

They tend to be the most effective
leaders we ever encounter.

Their words and actions
are congruent.

MOST EFFECTIVE FORM OF LEADERSHIP...
BY EXAMPLE - CIVIL RIGHTS MOVEMENT

FATHER THEODORE M HESBURGH, C.S.C, PRESIDENT EMERITUS OF THE UNIVERSITY OF NOTRE DAME

DR. MARTIN LUTHER KING, JR.

Honesty

Three Review Questions

1. What can be the impact of not honoring your word?

2. How does honoring your word increase your performance?

3. Where do you need to be more honest with your opinions?

My Thoughts on Honesty

Part 3

Being an Effective Leader . . . Responsibility

Responsibility

How do you view Responsibility?

Authority, Control, Power,
and Leader

or

Blame, Fault, Guilt, and Liability?

Responsibility

The only areas in your life you can influence are the areas you take responsibility for.

Making it Happen

Want to be a great leader? Take great responsibility.

How we view responsibility determines if we are the **victim** or the **victor**.

Responsibility = Making it happen

Making it Happen

The #1 leadership problem we have is responsibility.

Society teaches us to view responsibility as blaming others.

How We Create Victims

Making it Happen

People might not get all they work for in this world, but they must certainly work for all they get.
~ Frederick Douglass

Abdication of Accountability

- It's not my fault . . .
  it's my parents' fault.
- It's not my fault . . .
  it's the government.
- It's not my fault . . .
  it's my boss' fault.

The common language of a victim
is to deflect responsibility
and put it on others.

Frequent complainers are usually folks
that don't take responsibility.

Abdication of Accountability

Responsibility is not valued
in our entitlement society.

- Man sues fast-food
  restaurant for his obesity.

- Thief breaks into a store,
  falls, and sues the store.

- Child sits out of recess
  for acting up; teacher gets
  disciplined.

Abdication of Accountability

Most people are overworked in organizations today because there is a culture of . . .
abdication of accountability.

Good employee gets punished = more work and less time.

Bad employee gets rewarded = less work and more time.

Abdication of Accountability

If a manger feels that his organization doesn't have his back, accountability doesn't happen.

No organizational accountability is like running an adult daycare.

Leaders don't need to hold someone accountable; they need to teach them the power of responsibility.

Power in Responsibility

ARE YOU MANAGING AN ADULT DAYCARE DUE TO NO RESPONSIBILITY?

Abdication of Accountability

Some organizations even suffer from the "Union Mindset."

If ten hours is allotted for a job and you can do it in six hours . . . take the full ten hours.

Just do the bare minimum.

What type of example does this set for our family?

Power in Responsibility

Responsibility is at the heart of a person's pride and an organization's productivity.

Power in Responsibility

Instead of creating a culture of responsibility, organizations are sending people to time management seminars.

That's like putting a bandage on something that requires stitches.

Responsibility

When asked questions, is your natural
response to . . .

Respond like a victim?

Or

Respond like a victor?

Responsibility: making it happen.

No Power in Deflecting Responsibility

Victim Responses:

"I'm doing everything I can. We are in a tough industry/economy."

"If I had a better board, executive team, or sales director, I could . . ."

"I'm not in control/in charge."

"It's not my fault."

"My hands are tied."

Power in Responsibility

Victor Responses:

"I'll make it happen."

"It's possible . . ."

"How could we approach it from a different view?"

"There's got to be something we can do."

> We can choose to speak like a victim or victor.

Victim to Victor

At times, we all play the role of the victim with our language and behavior.

The question is . . . how long are we going to be the victim?

Once you can distinguish your behavior as being a victim, you can shift to being a victor.

SHIFTING FROM VICTIM TO VICTOR

THIS TRAFFIC IS GONNA MAKE ME LATE. I CAN'T BELIEVE THIS TRAFFIC. (VICTIM)

I WILL NEED TO LEAVE EARLIER NEXT TIME. (VICTOR)

Power in Responsibility

Being a Leader = Making it Happen

When we speak like a victim, we
eliminate our ability to create and
produce results.

You'll discover that being
100 percent responsible is part of the
equation in being able to reach **very
high levels** of effectiveness.

Power in Responsibility

In what areas of your life do you need to take on responsibility?

Health?
Blaming your work schedule or income for your health.

Wealth?
Blaming your situation, education, or upbringing for your income.

Happiness?
Blaming your co-workers and family members for your unhappiness or stress.

Power in Responsibility

The only situation or circumstance we can **influence** is what we choose to be responsible for.

There are three types of people in this world: those who make things happen, those who watch things happen, and those who wonder what happened.
~ Mary Kay Ash

Power in Responsibility

How responsible are you for **everything** that happens to you?

- 25 percent

- 50 percent

- 75 percent

- 100 percent

Most people are about 50 percent responsible. How do I know this?

Power in Responsibility

Because **they'll spend 50 percent** of their **day talking** about or trying to find **someone** who is responsible.

Can you believe what this person . . .

How effective would your organization be if *That's not my responsibility* was replaced with:

I'll make it happen.

Power in Responsibility

*Man must cease attributing his problems
to his environment, and learn again
to exercise his will and his personal
responsibility.*
~ Albert Einstein

Responsibility = Making it happen

The real impact of not choosing to be
responsible is that it makes us less of a
person.

Power in Responsibility

We diminish ourselves and our power when we put the blame on others or make excuses.

Ever notice that we are faster to make excuses than we are to try and solve something?

Think vs. React

Power in Responsibility

The **moment** an individual discovers
the power of taking 100 percent
responsibility is the time at which she
really understands that anything
is possible.

So . . . what's now possible for you?

Responsibility

3 Review Questions

1. What are the two ways to view responsibility?

2. How does being 100 percent responsible give you influence and power?

3. How do you implement a culture of responsibility where you work?

My Thoughts on Responsibility

Part 4

Being an Effective Leader . . . Generosity

Generosity

How do you view generosity?

I give enough.

Or

I give when I have a surplus.

Or

I strive to give at every opportunity I'm presented with.

Generosity

How we view generosity determines our interaction with it.

Society on Generosity

Do you have these thoughts?

I need to get that.

I wish I had that.

That person has that.

We are overwhelmed with advertisements that fuel our need to consume.

Society on Generosity

What would happen if we switched our desire for consumption to **contribution**?

Generosity

Generosity: Giving without expectation

Do we make sacrifices or do we sacrifice others?

There are numerous ways we can be generous daily and it has **little to do** with money.

Power in Generosity

Attention is the rarest and purest form
of generosity.

Power in Generosity

Nothing will hinder you more than thinking only about yourself.
~ Thomas à Kempis

Being Generous with Others

Being generous as a leader means we
must not be quick to judge or give up
on people.

Imagine if our parents just gave up on us
when they encountered
hard times?

SELF-SACRIFICING VS SACRIFICING OTHERS

THEY ARE COSTING US TOO MUCH. AND I'D LIKE TO KEEP MY LEXUS.

WHICH ONE ARE WE GONNA GET RID OF?

Self-Sacrifice vs Sacrificing Others

If we are going to call ourselves leaders,
we must ask more of ourselves than we
do of others.

Honor, Service, and Selfless?

Or

Self-Serving, Greedy, and Corrupt?

SELF SACRIFICE   VS   SACRIFICE OTHERS

What behavior does your environment demonstrate?

Being of Service

Being Generous

As soon as we sacrifice others or **label someone**

He's a jerk

Or

She's so bossy

Opportunities to be generous vanish.

Being Generous

Some people practice generosity only
when it is reciprocated.

What would happen if we weren't so
concerned with quid pro quo?

Giving Without Expectation

Generosity is not a response to what we
get . . . it is a
self-expression of **who we are.**

Generosity is also the quality or fact of
being plentiful or **large.**

It takes a big person to be loving and
understanding when around others who
are not.

Giving Without Expectation

Opportunities to be a big person:

Generous with our Understanding

Communicating with a co-worker who doesn't easily accept responsibility.

Generous with our Love

Demonstrating love and understanding for someone who is not giving it back.

Opportunities to be a big person:

Generous with our Patience
Communicating with a strong-willed person whose nature is to resist.

When we demonstrate our generosity toward someone, we express our hope for the possibility of a positive outcome.

We become BIG people when we are generous.

Become a Big Person

Becoming a BIG person also means we stop judging others by our thoughts, words, and actions.

Become a Big Person

*Really big people are, **above everything else**, courteous, considerate, and generous—not just to some people in some circumstances—but to everyone all the time.*
~ Thomas J. Watson (Chairman and CEO of IBM 1914-1956)

Become a Big Person

Nelson Mandela was a giant of a person. He forgave his captors who had imprisoned him for twenty-seven years.

Most of us are still holding on to something small that happened twenty-seven days ago.

Small people hold on to small events and live small lives.

Small people tend to **major in minor things**.

Become a Big Person

Forgiveness is a gift we give ourselves. It helps us become a bigger person.

*I've never heard anyone say
I wish I hadn't forgiven.*
~ Katerina Klemer

Our ability to **forgive** is proportional to our ability to **grow**.

Become a Big Person

Is there anything you're still
holding on to?

Become a Big Person

Go practice generosity and forgiveness.
You will free your mind from the
episodes of the past that you continue to
replay.

We get tired by what we
don't do. This continues to weigh on
our minds.

I know I need to talk with . . .
Go do it.

Become a Big Person

You shall love your neighbor
as yourself.
Matthew 22:39

What would happen if we actually
practiced this?

Giving Without Expectation

How about time vs money?

How generous are we
with our time?

DO WE BELIEVE THAT MONEY REPLACES TIME?

Power in Generosity

How can you be a generous
person daily?

Be generous with your patience for
your family/friends even when your
expectations aren't met.

It takes a giant of a person to constantly
give and
get nothing in return.

Daily Habit—Generosity

Be generous with your listening to a work colleague about the struggles they're dealing with at home.

Be generous with your **silence** by not having to respond or comment to everything you don't like.

Daily Habit—Generosity

Be generous in your understanding of
others by not labeling them.

Be generous with your appreciation of
what you have and what
others do for you.

You don't need to be a billionaire or own
a business to be generous.

Power in Generosity

In the giving of ourselves, we find the
greatest joy and fulfillment in life.

Power in Generosity

What opportunities do you have today
to be generous?

There is no exercise better for the heart
than reaching down
and lifting people up.
~ John Andrew Holmes

Power in Generosity

Could the highest form of
generosity be love?

Being Love

Love is patient, love is kind. It is not jealous, is not pompous, it is not inflated, it is not rude, it does not seek its own interests, it is not quick-tempered, it does not brood over injury, it does not rejoice over wrongdoing but rejoices with the truth. It bears all things, hopes all things, endures all things.
1 Corinthians 13:4-7

Love _____ all things.

Generosity

3 Review Questions

1. How quickly do we sometimes give up on people or label someone?

2. How much concern do we give quid pro quo?

3. Where can we give of ourselves more?

My Thoughts on Generosity

3 VALUES OF BEING AN EFFECTIVE PERSON

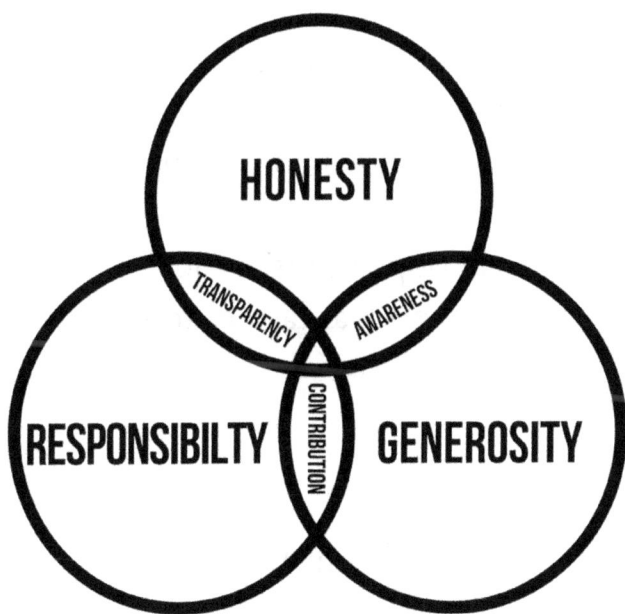

HONESTY

TRANSPARENCY

AWARENESS

RESPONSIBILTY

CONTRIBUTION

GENEROSITY

Eric Papp

Daily Scorecard

1. What promises did you fulfill today?

2. What did you take responsibility for that you've been projecting on others?

3. What opportunities did you take advantage of to be generous?

Thank You.
The world needs your leadership.

Scorecard for Managers

1. How are you doing in managing the promises of your people as opposed to managing them?

2. What type of proactive behavior ("I'll make it happen") are you observing?

3. How many honest conversations are you having?

Final Thoughts

Ways to Implement:

- Cut out the Daily Scorecard and hold yourself accountable.

- Share the book with your team and have them read it.

- Facilitate discussions on the book at work (lunch/learn).

- Use the Scorecard for Managers if responsible for a team.

- Examine current training programs and look for foundational problems.

- Keep the book visible so it serves as a reminder.

- Read the book a second time with a highlighter.

- Share the book with family and friends outside of work.

- Contact Eric and have him come speak to your organization.

IF EVERYONE PRACTICED THE 3 VALUES
(STANDARDS OF BEHAVIOR) YOU WOULDN'T SPEND
TIME IN THE WEEDS.